Flock Book

FLOCK BOOK

poems

Katie Umans

Black Lawrence Press
New York

Black Lawrence Press
www.blacklawrence.com

Executive Editor: Diane Goettel
Front cover design: Rebecca Maslen
Cover art: Grant Hanna
Book design: Pam Golafshar

Copyright © 2012 Katie Umans
ISBN: 978-0-9837945-2-3

All rights reserved. Except for brief quotations in critical articles or reviews, no part of this book may be reproduced in any manner without prior written permission from the publisher:
    Black Lawrence Press
    326 Bigham Street
    Pittsburgh, PA 15211

Published 2012 by Black Lawrence Books, an imprint of Dzanc Books
Printed in the United States

For my flock: My parents. Ryan & V.

ACKNOWLEDGEMENTS

Poems from this manuscript have appeared in the following publications, sometimes in slightly different versions, or under alternate titles:

Barrow Street	"Love Poem (Marrow)"
Bellingham Review	"Recipe"
Columbia: A Journal of Literature and Art	"Field's Chromatography"
Court Green	"Dream In a Time of War"
Forklift, Ohio	"Prodigal"
Fourteen Hills	"New Year's Eve, with Fever"
Indiana Review	"The Bathing Machine"
	"The Ostriches Take a Human Child"
The Tampa Review	"Lullaby for the Buffalypso"
Metamorphoses (an art book by Grant Hanna)	"Io, Tethered"
Michigan Quarterly Review	"Sestina to Undo the Little Albert Experiment"
Mid-American Review	"The Body Near Paintings"
	"Forecast"
"New Hampshire Poet Showcase"	"Ekphrastics"
Prairie Schooner	"Love Poem (in a False Tense)"
Salt Hill	"Ducdame, Ducdame"
	"Instructions to the Painter of Our Family Portrait"
Tuesday; An Art Project	from "Phobia Ladder"
	"Aquaphobia"
	"Cenophobia"
32 Poems	"The Gardens of Ninfa"

My heartfelt thanks are due to the English Department at Connecticut College, the MFA program at the University of Michigan, the Wisconsin Institute for Creative Writing, and the NH State Council on the Arts for support in many forms over many years. To the mentors who have shaped my poems and my very idea of poems, especially Charles Hartman, Thylias Moss, Linda Gregerson, Lorna Goodison, and Anne Carson. To my cohort and cohort-in-law at Michigan, the Wisconsinites of 2005-2006, the starving artist support group of the Brochecos. To those who read and cared about the poems in this book: Ryan Flaherty, Sarah Wolfson, Rae Gouirand, Darcie Dennigan, Rebecca Dunham, Colleen Abel, and many other thoughtful workshoppers. To Grant Hanna for use of his drawing "Flock Book" in the cover image. To Diane Goettel and Black Lawrence Press for selecting and publishing this manuscript.

CONTENTS

The First Biome / 3
The Bathing Machine / 4
(Ellis Bell is Emily Bronte.) (Acton Bell is Anne Bronte.) (Currer Bell is
    Charlotte Bronte.) / 5
The Synchronized Divers / 6

The Second Biome / 8
Io, Tethered / 9
New Year's Eve, with Fever / 10
Love Poem (Marrow) / 12

The Third Biome / 14
Dawn Simulation / 15
Forecast / 18

The Fourth Biome / 22
Field's Chromatography / 23
The Gardens of Ninfa / 27
Ducdame, Ducdame / 28
Phobia Ladder / 29

The Fifth Biome / 38
Ekphrastics / 39
The Body Near Paintings / 41

The Sixth Biome / 44
The Ostriches Take a Human child / 45
Prom Queen, Rose Garden / 48
Prodigal / 49

The Seventh Biome / 51
Instructions to the Painter of our Family Portrait / 52
"My Graft of a Cherry Tree on an Apricot Tree Did Not Take" / 53
Recipe / 55
Love Poem (In a False Tense) / 56

The Eighth Biome / 58
Sestina to Undo the Little Albert Experiment / 59
Lullaby for the Buffalypso / 61
Explanations on the Verge / 62

The Ninth Biome / 64
Magnet Turning / 65
Leavings / 67

The Tenth Biome / 69
Dream in a Time of War / 70

Notes & Attributions

FLOCK BOOK: a record of sheep or cattle, which includes information about parentage, pedigree, ownership, births, transfers, and deaths.

THE FIRST BIOME

Here the soil is human:
jutting with beets, potatoes, turnips—

    like elbows and knees of a rowdy crowd.

The people are clean
despite their peasant clothes. They hold their pale hands
to the sun and say   *toil*   *time*   *hardship.*

        Then slide shows of beet stains pass across their palms.

THE BATHING MACHINE

It made a country of women.

On the other side of the modest
contraptions, makeshift wooden changing rooms
wheeled out into shallows, they emerged

fleshy as sea lions on banks of rock, a frank display
under just the sun, hot as the eyelid
of one asleep and wading in a bawdy dream.

If a flap of bathing costume cleaved
to the wrong fork of a figure
it would be known only by the fish with bodies

taut as men's calves accidental under tables.
The plan was quarantine, of course, and yet
it assembled the most alluring archipelago—

sirens who'd hardly need to sing
the ships to them, a string of warm points
just off shore. Still what woman

here would summon wrecks
to splinter a seascape for now all hers—
or savor a graveyard of drowned men

in the waves, pulled uselessly under by desire.

(ELLIS BELL IS EMILY BRONTE.)
(ACTON BELL IS ANNE BRONTE.)
(CURRER BELL IS CHARLOTTE BRONTE.)

The suitors come hoping
our hands are white, and suppose
our knuckles are inked black, the house teased

by the skeletal breeze of quills—
so the goose-bumps raise on their arms.
The suitors come hoping

and for them we unfurl hushed anagrams—
    (Bronte: *be torn*
           riot us: Suitor: *trio us*)

but cannot stay still long enough. Restless, we
circle the perimeters of rooms
to find their acrostic meaning—leave

at the center the vases and tea sets,
the suitors' chalk bones
in their wing-back chairs. We hear

the Bells, industrious brothers, bellowing
our six-lunged solitude until we catch
its breath again. After all, all lives are trade.

A goose yields ten to twelve good quills—
plucked and sorted, put in hot sand to dry,
to harden in acids or alum. With two of us

to fall ill early and calculating
all three mortal, we will, between us,
yield some finite quantity of words.

THE SYNCHRONIZED DIVERS

To the side
of each
body: a body
like a novocained lip.

Arms raised
as if bound
to a headboard.
The breath

of both:
Flemish snow,
the outfield,
a watchery thick as briar.

THE SECOND BIOME

The sheen and cater,
the British voice says *it's a nature program, see...*

Press of the cat's body on the bed
        craters for us this grassy plain—

                no—footage of a grassy plain—

and so, thinking to stop suffering, I put a flock of zebras   on pause
        and lo, an errant lion follows me

        biting my ankles everywhere he should have caught a struggling body:
2 minutes 20 seconds, 50 minutes 22   and on and on—

                and now the dream marks time.

            Now the lion traipses everywhere
            behind me with the rage of a still savanna in his eyes
            while time follows, dragging its resentful tail.

And the people in the bed—how they mark each confiscated hunt is gentler.

And the people, if they woke now
would wake as in a hammock
    swaddled   but still swaying from some angry push.

IO, TETHERED

She had the stars lowing,
had the olives like a grove
of bitter, bitten thumbs fumbling.
She had the field close, sweating
its mustard and sugar, waiting
for her tongue and breath.
You think because she was a cow
she lost this art? For a moment
at the start there was panic's snowmelt
at the nape of her neck
and she felt in her solid lagging heart
what Zeus's wife must feel
whenever she is lifted off her husband's mind
like frost off grass. But then this passed.
She was not beauty but her body
was the size of beauty's danger.
Of course she sagged and grew fly-bitten.
Of course she smelled
more strongly of herself.
But she got her low-slung
heft floating in a pond's reflection
weightless as moonlight.
She buzzed like an aster flower.
If night was a dog at the throat of more night,
it calmed and lay down with her.

NEW YEAR'S EVE, WITH FEVER

In and out
of her match-struck

head, mirage
caryatids rise

to occasion: all
the steady architecture

of celebration,
wherein the hostess

shakes off
the puffin frown

of sickness, presents
light batter cakes atilt

with sugar roses, serves
chilled champagne

and strawberries until
everyone poses

beneath an ice sculpture
of the thitherto.

Instead she stays
Jonah-swallowed

in the sickbed, thinking
what a pity

love poems are—
admitting the heat

of another person.
The guests are amniotic

through the wall—
her body curved in

as a veined shrimp,
mind strewn as

a firmament.
Afield, afire,

a rising staircase
in the midnight countdown—

climbing back up
to the room

that says *rave*—
do not relinquish.

LOVE POEM (MARROW)

Even with all its sultry factorying,
this is the nunnery, the deepest silence—
the low-pitched hard snow, unwalkable,
where words and fingertips make least impression:
the skim of boat bottoms on fish bodies
in nearly iced canals. Here out of range
of sweetness, raunch, or worship
we're at hostage-in-negotiations, the introversion
whisked wherever brain flash
rockets body. No lacy bride—face nerved
and green as iceberg—slipper-foots
these aisles to her groom. Here the seethe
is spinster, here the carnal work
is marrying and marrying itself.

THE THIRD BIOME

It opens
        with a stomach of sunlight—

                        the lion dissolved away.

Here the shelled clear-cutters arrive,
a sporting look in their eyes, toothed saws at their sides.

        They carry pails of wax fruit, hang the fruit
        on the forest's trees and to the fumes
        of scorching plastic, grow ecstatic, tranced—

                the birds swing away from home and I turn the corner
                wondering, as always, if the stove is on—

                              and home is gone.

DAWN SIMULATION

Toward the end of the long winter
the sociologist, not the sun,
rose over us. He was there
to study the psychological effects
of a sky the spread, scuffed
texture of the mind, to study the effects
of the spring day fake-out last week.
Once he'd said: *They seem to have
a complex system of communication.*
Now he notes: *They say little.*

~

On the sidewalk, sometimes,
from inside a vast coat and hood—
a head might float up like a streetlamp
and say *hello*—but that was rare.
Some houses had swingsets,
which proved children.
But right now they proved only wind.
The sociologist went on TV. He said:
They pool under ice. They try but they cannot.

~

There was a harvest on the other channel.
During commercials you could order
a bushel of apples with the toothmarks of nubiles.
Some even got a premium channel
with sunstroke from which you could,
you'd swear, smell hot tar.

Their homes were heated and for a bit
they forgot that outside it was winter
and paced their living rooms in short sleeves
feeling just a vague displacement
just a vague sense of being the goldfish.

~

The Light Box for the treatment
of Seasonal Affective Disorder blazed
on the morning tabletop.
It had no Red Giant tantrums.
Few watched the sociologist speaking.
Who were we to change the world?
We didn't know ourselves at all.
Our personalities were atmospheric—
like opera music played outside Italian restaurants
to lure in customers. Who were we
to know when he said *they* that he meant *us*?

~

On campuses, the outrage
posters burned with color, like an autumn.
We walked close by them.
We caught their magic marker light,
like heatlamp. We caught their smell
of strawberry and brain burn, factory lemon.
We felt incubated, ready for naps.

~

It was not all setting. If pressed
we could recall some dialogue—

a loved one's voice across the room
responding to the sociologist's phone survey:

>"Strongly agree."
>"Strongly disagree."
>"Very worried."
>"Somewhat worried."

FORECAST

It is a gray day, one to stay home and write helplessly *father father father*
in the margins of Plath, an endless rain the gutters take and shape.

I know planes are lifting off from drizzled-under runways. I should feel them
in my body like a needle and white thread drawn through the tough skin of
        fingertips.

Who is on the planes? All the loved ones—and shouldn't I feel them
as they fly into the heavy clouds? Or are we only free to feel the dead above us?

~

Well, brain, mushroom cloud over all my body's bright
impudent courage—where will we not go today?

When are we muscle and when are we muscle
striving and when do we grow legs to crawl up out of sludge?

~

The clouds don't last, and there is heat to worry us.
As a test to see what I can face I ask myself: *Do you understand*

you do not love the sun? You love the 8.3 light minutes that divide you from it.
Do other loves grow sad for being more or less exact than that?

When Icarus flew at the sun he took his father (and don't all fools
strap someone into their front seats) but he did not get far.

He swerved halfway just as the breath of Icarus
went soft and yeasty as a baby at the breast.

He grew self-conscious and he tipped his wings to turn
and knew that it was not his place or story.

But how many light minutes from such myth?
I feel no spark or scorch from it.

~

In the School of Imagistic Climate Studies
it's suggested that, for mercury to fall, a thousand

women must be hired to take the silver earrings
from their ears at once. First their lobes will cool

like arctic banks and then their sheets, their rooms—
and then the sun will put us down.

I'm thinking I'll take back the gray, sling tragic Russian novels
on my back and run through rain to translate them.

~

If you sit across from someone with a sun-warm, flown-in orange
between you on the table, you may believe that rivalry is who will get the fruit.

It's not. You break the fruit in sections. Rivalry is who pulled off the peel
in one smooth motion so it lies, transformed into a glammed-up curl,

a sunlit path with gate swung shut. A healed peel or a hatch of leaves
across a hole will seldom yield a captive, but some questions do fall in

as we sit by to wait. Like: would it be one-upmanship if, reading
a friend's play called *The Lost Sheep*, I wrote a play I called *The Dead Sheep*

or would it be more of a boast to write *The Sheep Beside Me Sleeps*
(near monologue of fleece and moonlight)?

~

The woman who does weather on the radio has the same head cold
as the young reporter flown to cover Middle East affairs.

Once romances didn't get so far. The fishers could not leave
their shores, the marbled ocean touched with the same froth

that touched their fishwives' leather mouths, the squalls and tempests
hitting both at once so that a curse the fishwife uttered

could take down a mast or send a heap of scales and flesh
into her husband's net. Kissing his wife, he tasted nothing

farther on the map than salt and local current.
Sometimes a harbor or a secret inlet. Sometimes a lost man

from his own crew and the strange town he'd since washed up in—
but then only its public markets. Lips were not horizons.

Now the fast food chains are everywhere, the teenager
who hands out paper bags of food at drive-through windows—

she's of two hemispheres—one arm stretched out goose-bumped into cold,
the other hot and pinpricked by the splattered fry grease.

THE FOURTH BIOME

The fevers rise: verdure of youth, sun

                                        on everything:

broad leaf and sugar cane

                        making the abundant animals sweat.

          Their mouths are mossy trying for some word—orchid—

                                      for some strenuous word to bloom.

FIELD'S CHROMATOGRAPHY
—*after the color guide of 1869*

1.

Mr. Field walks with a cane (granular
brown on his palm), white-haired,
splintering. Every day a slower
stalking of his pillow.

       Puddle-ducks
lap a spring thaw,
parasols flap up.

Mr. Field, the people nod. Ice is moving.

2.

How he had craved gloom's opposite
so long ago (boastful drake,
putting on dark hat, tweed coat,
dancing his way out of them,

       eyelids sealed
tight for the streaks, flashes
like fruit on the tongue)

not knowing he would find its bright center.

Oh gloom, he'd said
accidentally to the dark horse,
jumping astride.
He'd taken the reins (oily

      brown on his palms)
and dug his heels in hard.
Everything could be pressed on.

Summer would be autumn, aflame, deep in.

3.

Whenever he walked, he looked
for lusters. The carp in the pools
(when they swam out from his reflection
as he longed to do) were fissures

      in that ordinary self,
having thrashed their forms
free of him, a tweed embankment.

He was a man of little sheen—and less without them.

4.

In his guide to colors
he worded carefully
his new orange pitched toward red
ideal for bird throats, blazes,

        conspicuous flowers.
It is my job, he'd told his love, *to look
at other women's dresses.*

The sun cast a wan almond-flesh light.

The puddle ducks are green,
she had replied, *with lovely, complex
feathers. My eyes are rarest malachite,
my hair burnt umber or sienna.*

        She'd embroidered her gown
with spice-golds and crimson. She'd twirled
in her parlor for hours, for him

(the chaperone dizzy with spinning beside her).

5.

When, during their long courtship, he slipped
midstream in reverent talk of love
suggesting hues of flesh
and cheeks of heightened pinks

        she grew as
flabbergasted as she could
in corset. She flamed off.

The china orange vermilion bowl grew ruined in his kitchen

easing from its darkening fruits (some
solidarity, some link of beauty
going) and, since, his mind had painted
every woman in this shade—through gown

        or headdress, exaggerated
hair itself and, yes, by throat
when she insisted on herself

as poignant bird, by fact of flight, by fact of nesting elsewhere.

Mr. Field, the people nodded at his
solitary frame for years. They moved
in blurs, in faded floral mass.
So often a clear rain was in his eyes.

THE GARDENS OF NINFA

In a pope's once-barren garden, sprung up
from alkalines once buried deep as saints,
buff beauty roses now rebuff
the sweep of long-gone robes.
A nice day for a departed soul to stroll
in bee-buzz, in what 200,000 gold florins
once bought and mercenaries seized
for no payment at all until centuries later—
out of ruins, out of a curse, out of
a cloud of malaria—climbed three
to claim it—Ada first, then daughter
Donna, finally Margeurite—clematis vine
slunk slyly up a dry-trunk family tree.
Rustle of the phantom pope hustling
through lavender, his long robes catching
its perfume as he heads to the stone sculptures,
to the birch grove, where things stay still
and white, as in a girlhood, before
the women gardeners went shamelessly
to seed, their skirts hiked up
to dig, with dandelion spindles thrusting
any-old-wish up. So he arrives, sachet
for the odorless birches. "Corraggio!"
cries Marguerite, today at work, "Corragio, ghost,
for wafting back up to your heaven scented so.
Take raspberries before you go!"

DUCDAME, DUCDAME

> Amiens: What's that 'ducdame'?
> Jaques: 'Tis a Greek invocation to call fools into a circle.
>
> —As You Like It

Mooncalves, quilting—what comfort
can you make? And for whose deathbed?
Parable of the careless bricklayer:
setting bricks down on a map, he lost the world.
Parable of his unseen meadow growing over.

Inside your chests are bent-down branches laden.
Parable of apple-picking: it cannot be done
without allusion, so you have left
the orchard shamed. Yes, fall into
another fish-on-ice nap, wait for spring.

Parable of the first day of May: a girl
miles from the maypole twines white ribbon
round herself like spider silk. Cook your stew
for one: scrubbing potatoes (dungeon doors),
celery (rained-out canyons). And what for meat?

Parable of the hermit cannibal.
You make a wish. The wind says: *what a tiny wish*.
Parable of the mosaic: missing piece.
You intend. The wind says: *gone already*.
Though you still feel it skitter on the roof.

PHOBIA LADDER

Monster sweetie, be a good monster and just speak once.

        Aquaphobia   (fear of water)

Coral is the lace of caught girl divers.
Yes sea wasps poison prawns

and parrot-beaked the blue-ringed octopus
injects its prey but they are just

the bodied forms of deadliness.
 Pour it. See in a clear jar:

your breathlessness, your death
suspended, poised

as in formaldehyde. I spoon
the liquids to my lips,

no more than I need. See by the lake
the posture of the homes

grows rigid. They are nervous.
They stay up all night.

        Bathaphobia   (fear of bathing)

It's not the water. It's what it takes.
Tub tinged the translucent sallow

of the orchard peach with its light fuzz.
Estrangement—see old hairs,

old residues exhale the fallen *someone else*.
Cruel kingdom: great cerebral head

presiding over these topographies,
these miles of debauching towns.

In the temple drawing *Man Assisted
by Two Women to Wash Long Hair*

the artist understands that we are barely
conjured stuff. Although the man's idolized

hair is muscled as an arm, the women
bathers' breasts are careless C's

slapped on at angles, water
an eraser rubbing at the lines.

        Coitophobia   (fear of sex)

When I was born, I traced
back to my parents'

dry skin: the passion-cratered
bed, lava, heat that flows

to cold shelves. What goes
un-played as hands perform

their trombone slide
to seek those few pure notes of nerve?

And here I've found the barren clef
(what you call pleasure)—

the screen's cold-lighted rooms,
its small, bald-bodied girls,

some man who grimly moves
each one away

and toward him like a violinist
rosining a bow.

        Chrometophobia   (fear of money)

Faces rising up from green
like sonograms: one body

quicksanded in hermit's aspic.
A worried fingering of tea leaves.

New currencies? New tinted landscapes
with the same electric fence

around them—same smell of handshakes
between the living and the dead.

Cibophobia (fear of food)

The dead all die
full-stomached. Platefuls pull

them down, rocks in the kitten-bags.
The king has a mutinous taster,

shy curls like mold. He bends his head
in false humility. Flesh metes out

its coup of maggots. Potatoes lift
bits of your eventual grave

into your throat. The etymology
of *sustenance*: endurance.

Of *endurance*: to bear. To bear a weight,
a wait—this never lifting off

from earth. All food is haunt
as atoms of rot reshape to ripeness.

See the fruits—they grow, un-tethering
from branches, never from time.

Ailurophobia (fear of cats)

Full of themselves,
throats crammed with fur,

their sand tongues rattling ready
to plow into me for that patch

of sun: the heart. They eat
elevator music, piped in meats

but want my rich breath of real cream.
Magnolia bleaches my yard like eyes.

        Brontophobia   (fear of thunder)

The sky a plate, then
the sky a plate

hairlined then the sky
as shards, then—what

shards will birth.
Like worms sliced

they fission—the new
perhaps no plate at all.

Vivisected, the incision
made. The surgeon's

throat is cleared. Forceps
will next descend.

Cenophobia   (fear of empty spaces)

Once, inside a salt-
and dirt-hemmed train

I saw a warehouse
in blue pilot light

and recognized it
as the back

of my own throat.
I clicked to take

its picture, make
it twin to silence

I had swallowed
all my life.

It screams there
when I wake it.

It screams for me.
I put my hands

in my lap. I turn
my nerves on

like every light
in the house.

       Xenophobia   (fear of foreigners)

A blank cloth
may be blank

or may be soaked
in ether. Or: see the way

my uninvited guest
raises his body up

to stand the way
a teakettle is lifted onto heat.

       Venustraphobia   (fear of beautiful women)

Galapagos finch, beauty
is no staircase but a timeline.

That most perfect tropic
in whose branches you can preen

and sunbathe has long since
sailed me off its surface,

origami wreck,
a practicing of folds.

Kakorrhaphiophobia   (fear of imperfection)

With my scythe
I could bring down the harvest

but that I am in a minefield.
Mine (of course) a field

of letters—the lifelong
sting of spelling bee.

THE FIFTH BIOME

A man enters the dream alone
        wash your pioneer hair   he says
that I may bury my face in it

    and in all first kisses in books, the girl—

        -tastes like roses and smells like soap
        -tastes like peppermint and smells like rain
        -tastes like gum and smells like honeysuckle

    which means she never smells like herself, never tastes like herself.

So I am grateful to the man.
    He has flipped through The Atlas, a land surveyor, an appraiser.

In the morning, we will rinse this out with mouthwash, but now—

    What flock sweats in the room   where two people sleep
        and one woman washes her dream hair   for another man?

    What flock charges where the dream of betrayal breaks
        kaleidoscopic   in a mind   and makes no picture?

    To the eyes we are all swan-glide through sleep.

EKPHRASTICS

The brown house in yellowed landscape
is pure exercise in architecture,
portrait of land's thirst.

(What you cannot see:
a homestead woman
stands behind the house,

killing sage chickens
with a shotgun. The painter
hates her heat,

her bloodied hands
and patience, but she hates
her hunger more.)

~

The woman at toilette:
a sheep white wisp of paint
whose thoughts have always

rested lightly in her mind
like tortoise combs in piled-high hair—
she wanted nothing more or less

than what her watcher wanted
from her: hollow
of her throat, a face

to turn to mirrors, soft
anticipation of
the evening's entertainment.

(She did not want an infant
by her dressing table, the painter
sure to render it

the frail gray-white
of garlic with its
purple underbleed.)

~

The latest model arcs
on the divan.
(At home, in kitchen light,

the painter's wife
peels a thick neck
of butternut for supper.)

The painter puts
the model's nakedness
into the horse's eye,

the one that's flickering
with nervous ignorance beneath
the hero braced for battle.

THE BODY NEAR PAINTINGS

Egon Schiele's nudes are bruised
and fish-twisting in their paint.

A woman stops near them,
stilled by her attention to the nudes,

standing in the gallery—still
things not happening in the painted bodies

happen in her. Her blood circulates.
It happens she ovulates. She grinds her teeth.

Her heart beats. Her shoulders are tight.
Neurons brighten as she observes the paintings.

The blood of the models is gone,
what Egon said to them in his studio is gone.

And in her abdomen—a pinch that's right there.
She must admit she feels the urge

to take the nudes from their bourbon dusks,
their flypaper beds, like invalids to fresh-air parks.

Except, if they were flesh, to touch them
in their sprawl and spoil would be consummation.

When his bodies touch, they cling,
they decay into each other. Or loll and drift.

They smell. They do. Just to look at.
They are to sex what compost is to food, she thinks.

Squint and their leanness makes
the slats of crates in which animals fatten,

the blades of slaughter. She stays
in place and lets the bodies settle

into her like garden stakes. A vine shivers up.
She stares into their cell-blank rooms

as phantom scenery fills in behind them—
wet hay and thin strays, nest spill and dropped egg,

steel wool and barbed wire, sprung spring
and church spire, rat hands and coiled glands,

bent hangers and void amber.
Hindering the artist is a crime. So Egon said once:

jailed, in lust, burning, hindered—
and sick again with a body.

THE SIXTH BIOME

Odd that next, instead of arctic, we get—the Queen
holding ice cubes, each with a scene inside:

>Jamestown with its replica ships and plaques

>the racehorses of Kentucky

>astronauts of Maryland

>and soldiers of Washington

>Betsy Ross's head bent in work.

The Queen burbling
with amusement and sympathy,

>her fingers getting cold
>>until the sun rises, a locket with her picture in it

>>>and everything goes liquid.

THE OSTRICHES TAKE A HUMAN CHILD

—*When a pair of ostriches bearing young meets another pair, the parents will fight and the winning pair will be parents of both pairs' offspring.*

Come sit at the table. We'll slice you an apple.

    See the pieces of fruit are as white as your throat.
        See the pieces of fruit are as splayed as your hands.

Are you feeling at home yet? (If you wait they will brown.)

    We will spread all the slices with thick peanut butter.
        We want you to stay. This is lake mud to hold you.

Now watch through the water as through a warped window:

    see there in slow motion your legs that can't move.
        My, aren't you stubborn!—you're a stuck straw to suck though—

that lakewater taste of you, strange and removed.

        (We will have to drink more of that
            till it tastes good.)

Our necks are the waterpipes threading your rooms.

    And isn't that sweet how all day you will live
        in the sound of our swallowing—tense when you're foolish

and loving when good and stern when it's needed (you'll know

> what you've done). Is this feeling like home yet?
> Is it feeling like love?

The flightbirds need stiff down, but ours can be soft.

> It's for nothing but nesting.
> It can't push us off.

We've been hats, we've been leather in grandmothers' closets.

> We've been dusters that wiped all the dust from your shelves.
> We've been farmed for our offal, rich mineral spread.

We're brawn and big eyes and our legs are for racing.

> Our skirts are pushed up and we wince when we're bridled
> (but don't worry, your legs are not long enough yet).

And you can't grind a pebble in that soft, chalky throat.

> It is too full of talk.
> (It is probably broken.)

You're too large to be hatched, but we sat with your parents

> and turned over your life that was smooth as an egg
> and we won fair and square and we took you away.

And you felt just like velvet when we first touched your skin.

> (When we took you away, that's when we took you in.)
> We will buy you a bunk bed and smooth back your hair.

We'll unlock and restock you with organs like ours.

    And we'll puff up your feathers
        until they are there.

No parents at all—that is worse, is it not? No strong kicks to protect you

        when predators show. No umbrella above you to shade you from sun.
          (We could leave you in sand. You could learn how to run.)

PROM QUEEN, ROSE GARDEN

It's so I'd be a beautiful blur.
If I ran. If things got moving,
which they won't. But really it's because
if not there'd be no *theme*.
Things lovely and blooming—got
the picture?—the one to put forever
on the mantle? It's like that poem
from English class where girls
are gathering their rosebuds,
which will fade, but they're
the flowers really, really dying.
That "To the virgins, to make much of"
much is made of. Not by me.
Blood warm and warmer, warmest. Sorry,
but I'm not meant for a single vase.
I've gone to prom before.
Forget the poem. This garden—
it's just like being in my brain the last
three months, my brain gone wildflower
with its scattered gowns. I've tried on
every color here. Crows, jittery
as low-rung girls, surround me
and I'm sick of waiting and of photo ops
and standing by the birdbath. I wish
the limo wouldn't tarry. I'm dying here.

PRODIGAL

Do not, for a moment, put me
on the doorstep. First consider
how oddly tender is this current pairing:
me and my freedom, like the massive man
in leather walking his dinner roll of a dog.

Already I know the outcome. Nights I wake
hover-crafting homeward, suddenly four feet
above my sheets, my pillow. I tie
my arms and legs to the bedposts,
lie with rocks on my belly. Still I can see it:

the *Welcome Home* banner waving, my whole
family dissonant, blood-ready as a hog farm.
Some nights I'm lucky. My home north,
I dream south. My faithful llama
gulps whatever ocean lies before us

and we walk forward onto clean sand,
absolute absence. Oh my llama,
Rodriguez, my spirit and bulk of phlegm!
How he never looks back at me
with my own face. Slick bivalves, long oozing

only to the walls of their pinched shells
fall open at his four feet, parching.
Momentarily they join into one muscle,
a ligament lurching to quiet. On this conveyor
we are carried: anywhere but.

THE SEVENTH BIOME

Here in the emptied pasture, tufts
               of belly-wool caught on the fence
     give off the shaky scent of the barely over.

The low, dragging count
     could not get even
the woman in the mattress commercial to sleep.

        In the margins of registry, the parasites bury deep.
            This is where mothers roam away and a nervous shedding sets in.

        If you are pure, carry the genes, thawing in the heat of you like ice,
        carry them off from the white blaze of lambing.
                           If not, let them melt away—

            The man must have stood in the pasture, tending the sheep.

The field is mustardy and close
and draws your nose   your teeth and tongue.

But step up to the other bounty—   step up to the table of ribbons.

INSTRUCTIONS TO THE PAINTER OF OUR FAMILY PORTRAIT

A wallpaper, repeating. Make us
smile crescents, fresh-baked. In the early dusk,

dinner's afterburn, mound its wreckage soft on plates.
Leave the blankets forging our shapes,

the unwatered ancestors tenacious as cacti
on the beige wall. We are an accordion folding

and unfolding to tune. Oh goodsnap
of elastic things: everyone home.

If an ant fattens on the tile, it is by our crumbs.
Oh bellyaches meltable as snowdrift, boildown of tea.

We are warm, tumble-dried. Give us
our good square and we will fill it with the greenest grass,

with the salt of birth and family swimming. These fingernails we have
to hook with. Your brush, and our hair it cannot comb.

"MY GRAFT OF A CHERRY TREE ON AN APRICOT TREE DID NOT TAKE"

Once, hearing the clink of a neighbor's plates
        through a summer screen, I joined

her life—all from across the way, from
        the clink of her dinner plates.

I was no beetle-face against the holes.
        I was inside, my hands smelled of her

dish-soap. What intimacy can a screen
        not afford the willing, un-provincial traveler?

In my compounding state I would gladly live
        alone: *bookworm* in a *houseboat*, garden

blooming with *moonflowers*, enjoying a meal
        of *peppercorns* crusted on *catfish*. For dessert

a cobbler of my *cherrycots*. Blank
        buttock of the apricot, tight pucker

of the cherry: every fruit bowl a lechery.
        My rheumy brain can't help but drip

these juices: scion into groove, torrid as gardening
        never is. All I know is that I thought the plan

was unimpeachable. (Ha. Peach! Now that would make a threesome.)
        For who would wish to be himself

from cuff to cap or hem to hairline (if a her)?

Say I am overcome. Say I am rash.

I'll tuck you down into your narrow beds
                and, so unhinged, I'll work these hinges on.

RECIPE

> *Taste or smell ginger and a passionate*
> *love affair is in the cards, but it won't last.*
> — The Dream Dictionary

> *Gingerbread is a sign of a family party.*
> — The Dream Dictionary

It just might be:
the good domestic life
warm aftertaste of piquancy
and bite, the baking in
and gentling of what was
scorch and provocation
in the mouth. In the kitchen—
the room daily blackened
and cleaned like a confessional—
the only way to safely capture
is to make ingredient, to soften
the roaring on the tastebuds
with refined white breaths
of flour, fusing these with
mild molasses, corpulent
cuts of butter, until
the spicy waft of winter bread
pulls children up
from bed like smoke.

LOVE POEM (IN A FALSE TENSE)

Thankfully a whole town lies
between us. All daylight flints
the pavement: a match
that strikes the thought
of the night's walk
to you again and again
in my mind: each
imagined walk one lamp lit
along a street
from atop invisible stilts.
I do not hesitate to
navigate in such indelibles.
But if in recollection
there can be no new gesture
I stand still
as a street under snowfall.
The streetlamps strain through.
Here I am, still on my way.

THE EIGHTH BIOME

And how could this be an empire? It is so gentle.

The hollow, the cranny incarnate.

We could stay here forever.

        Hollow of fate's instep   cranny between   its neck and shoulder.
               It does not matter   this place to burrow.

Now piccolo tunes are buttons down our uniforms

and we unpack
        our feast on checkered cloths.

And since checkered cloths are gameboards   we must be cautious.

Corn kernels too
run the length of our uniforms   buttoning down our insides.

We lick orange snackdust from our fingers
        like a pollen,
               make a mobile of bees to hang over the park.

        And the bees fixed to their spots
are buttons down our uniforms

though they come unbuzzed

     in the twilight   the twill   the cloth we're weaving   this quiet goodwill.

SESTINA TO UNDO THE LITTLE ALBERT EXPERIMENT

The so-called "Little Albert Experiment" involved teaching an infant to fear various objects and animals by hitting a loud bar behind his head upon his exposure to them. There was no time for the conditioning to be reversed before he was taken home.

March, 1920. Watson is un-caging the bunnies, the monkey, the rat, the dog, and laying down the Santa mask. Watson is in love with Rosalie, his assistant, the woman who has helped him to condition baby Albert to fear all of the above, plus Watson's wooly hair and cotton—all white softness put before him. After this, Rosalie will marry Watson. For now they exchange just accidental touches, discreet gazes.

And when the bar crash-bangs, when the bunnies level their red gazes on him and his thumb is pulled from his mouth to be placed on the rat's ropey tail, is Albert learning too to fear this budding love of Rosalie and Watson? At home, seeing his father gently touch his mother's arm, will he hear Rosalie's soft sigh as she is touched, and shriek? During family picnics, seated under
    clouds white
and wooly as Watson's hair as he leans in for a kiss, will Albert

feel the world bending over him in sinister conspiracy? What of when Albert meets a woman he could love but for the way she gazes at him knowingly, as over heads of unsuspecting children? The white chalk grinds down on blank slate. Flash of the monkey, the rat, the dog, the beard, the cotton and smoking newspapers. Flash of Rosalie smiling at the smiling, white-bearded Santa under which looms grim Watson

with his own hair spilling out the top. Even without Watson's
broad hand hitting the bar, we know a bit of being Albert.
A bar crash-bangs and we open our arms for our Rosalie,
our Watson. We watch for our affections mirrored in a gaze,
learn to fear another's death by touching their skin—just as, in that room, the rat's
thick tail rubs dread on Albert's hand. We fear: creatures with white

fur, newspapers, wooly hair, beards. Or: the empty pillow's white
beside us—the lover gone, the lover out of love. So bring back Watson,
curious and eager to map the human state. Bring back the bunnies, the rat,
the dog, the monkey and the rest. We must un-condition. We must empty Albert
of his fears. This time the bar is silent as he meets the humble gaze
of each and every animal. The bar is silent as he's held by Rosalie.

The bar is silent as his mother takes him from the arms of Rosalie,
nudging his soft lips open for his thumb, wrapping him in swaddling of white
cotton. Behind the one-way glass, a team of scientists gazes
with approval as the boy is held and rocked. Among them is Watson.
All falls into nativity tableau: the beasts warm a circle around Albert,
his hand lain in mild, indifferent love on the back of the nearest rat.

LULLABY FOR THE BUFFALYPSO

> The Buffalypso is a hybrid of a water buffalo and dairy cow developed in
> Trinidad in the 1940s to yield low-cost meat. Its name is a cross between
> buffalo and calypso, the music from its island of origin.

Hush now. This world is mostly waiting.

I will tell you, miracles are what nature cannot be
trusted with even the seed of. They are not
what scattered the wet grains from the brewery

on the plantation ground, fattening the water buffaloes
to sudden health, not what took note
and pulled the best bulls out: straightest top lines,

strongest loins, refined heads, good rumps, with meat
down to the hocks. Meaning, a great weight
holds you to the pasture. Why must you hear

some god bend down to whisper *welcome,*
my lost pets, my good soldiers, welcome my
more-than-what-you-are when I have given you

grass, eyelids opening on all there is to see
up to the hills, the lungs to fill and empty and
fill again, four ankles that will twist and heal.

Sleep now, hurried ones. Sleep in your own bodies,
also in the good idea you are. In the morning,
the sun will shine on you as on anything.

EXPLANATIONS ON THE VERGE

You're asleep: danger glass-cased
behind your eyes. When you're lifted hot
from the fluids, that is called waking.
A music strains homeward where home
is a house being cleaned and everyone pushed
outside for the mopping. Hearing a music
you wake (the waking a foliage turning in you
where you were a green, green grove).
Wake and you are the ocean beached, a rag-doll
prodded for posture. Wake and this is called
breakfast and it tastes clear. Wake and you must
tip the brainwater back into the rut (and that
is called worry or that is called thought).
Sleep and you smell like almonds in milk
and the milk never needs to be poured away.

THE NINTH BIOME

Morning in the window—
the dream is deciduous.

    It begins its shed: antlers,
    leaves, pigment, smoke.

I have an apron-full.

    When the earth lags and trips,
    I must feed it its own slough:

        antlers, leaves, pigment, smoke

    until it rises slowly, in a crouch:

        moss, heath, shrub, lichen   the doubled-over plants, the permafrost,
                                            the ache in the joints.

        The man says
        wash your caretaker hands
        that you may run them over me.

MAGNET TURNING

Early winter:
snow soon to fall, pressing
like the marks of ribbons you have taken
from your hair to sleep.
Switch places.
Let me sleep while you write this.

~

At the cold beach
where a bonfire burned
away you pick up stones,
their blank stares.
A man you meet there
owns a Persian rug store
which is overstocked
so that he feels like every day
he's standing in a backed-up tub,
even the windows blocked with rugs
like lizards on warm rock
and in this darkness we must talk
to keep awake.

~

A chief in equatorial Africa
once dreamed he went to England.
He woke up, ordered
a wardrobe of European clothes
and called his friends to gather
and hear tales about his trip.

~

Frenchman André dreamed that he was in
the Reign of Terror when his headboard
fell across his sleeping neck.

~

A Cherokee was treated for a snake bite
after dreaming the snake's bite.

~

When Dali napped, he'd place a tin plate
on the floor, then sit beside it
in a chair and hold a spoon
above until he dozed, awaking
by his sabotage. He claimed refreshment,
claimed no exportation
at the next meal's clatter. Should we try?
You are growing perforated, bending to the break.

~

A charm for your image-gathering.
Be this: the rip in the sleep-walking gown.
Be ache of sealed chimney in an old house
where a new family lives.
And go on, keep moving—
you are still on the cold beach.

~

Begin with a scene. Early winter:

LEAVINGS

Deep in the dream, a negligence—
a detail you won't bring to waking
or repair: carpets unthreading themselves,
planets unattended losing their dyes,
blanching and slendering like jawbreakers
in the quiet place of undiscovery. No matter
how abroad you are, you go on breathing
just the bedroom's warmed, domestic air.
The fox connotes a rival. Instead you've
conjured up white foxes slumbering
in snow: the dream of the good citizen.
To witness moth holes in material speaks
of sadness in a family, but outside the moths
are their own sadness, pressing pauper faces
to your screen. In the solvent sunlight,
you'll live with what the window frames,
no question: the tree both view
and breach of view, the falling leaves its surfeits
and its forfeits—so surged with color,
so damp and downcast.

THE TENTH BIOME

Where we, as bedmates, must meet the eyes of one musk-ox

    its guard-hair hanging to the ground,
        shy as the high school punk at the back of the room,
            its molt like a rot—

but the ring the musk-ox form
around their calves: the ring is what we'd like to wake inside—

    and we must meet the eyes to gain admittance.

        and though herd-talk is   a bloody talk
            within a circle   we would speak it
        we would gash the land with it   we would let it scab.

We must hope for wolves, not hunters. Against hunters, the circle is futile.

We must stand the squalid smell,
the circle's inward sweat and grassy spit—

        dream's doppelganger of this scentless moat
        of winter slush around our house.

DREAM IN A TIME OF WAR

In the dream, people came for a re-enactment. In the re-enactment, two people climbed a mountain. When they reached the top, one told the other that it wasn't a mountain. There was no alternative. It wasn't that it was a hill or that the mountain was eroding. It wasn't that they were transcending the physical world, or in a distant country where mountains were called by other names. It was not a mountain—that was all. Each time, the one told was devastated. The crowd stood and said nothing. It was sad. They had come for sadness. They could believe it—that what they stood on was not a mountain—but it was hard to endure the sorrow of the person told, the way she stood, windless, as if she'd known that she was being led to something brutal. It felt like someone saying to another in the midst of a wedding or over the light of birthday candles: you will die. This was a re-enactment. No one had been there the first time, when this had really happened. Many people came to see this scene but most could bear it only once. I was watching it a second time. I knew how quietly the one to be told would be led up, knew that even though she did this every day, she had no idea of what letdown awaited. People did not come for violence. No one was pushed. The rocks at that summit were not even sharp, not even hot in the sun. People came for disappointment. It was terrible each time, and people came to bear that. There were children there. They had to learn. It's hard to say what we descended from.

NOTES & ATTRIBUTIONS

~ "The Bathing Machine": In the Victorian era, bathing machines "were bathhouses on wheels that rolled into the water and had an opening facing the sea... They allowed [a woman] to change into her bathing suit in private, and then demurely walk right into the water without fear of shocking those on the beach." —*The New York Times*, July 18, 2004.

~ "(Ellis Bell is Emily Bronte)...": The title is a biographical note written on September 19, 1850 for the 2nd edition of Emily Bronte's *Wuthering Heights*. The italicized phrases in the poem are anagrams of surrounding words.

~ "Ducdame, Ducdame": The epigraph is from Shakespeare's *As You Like It*. There is no record of the word "ducdame" outside of the play. Jaques' own definition (which he volunteers just as his companions form a circle around him) is all that is available. One speculation (from a footnote in the Norton edition) is that the term derives from either the Welsh "Dewch da mi," meaning "come hither," or a Gypsy phrase meaning "I foretell."

~ The first line of "Phobia Ladder" is from Shakespeare's *The Tempest*.

~ "The Body Near Paintings": The italicized phrase is attributed to Egon Schiele, 1912.

~ "My Graft...": The title is taken from a lithograph by Honoré Daumier, displayed at the University of Michigan Museum of Art.

~ "Sestina to Undo the Little Albert Experiment": The Little Albert Experiment was conducted in 1920 at Johns Hopkins University by John B. Watson and Rosalie Raynor.

~ "Lullaby for the Buffalypso" takes its material and epigraph from *Spirit of Enterprise: the 1990 Rolex Awards*.

~ "Magnet Turning": Some anecdotes referenced are from the research book *Some Must Watch While Some Must Sleep* by William C. Dement.

Katie Umans lives in New Hampshire with her husband and daughter. Her poems have been published in *Prairie Schooner, Crazyhorse, Columbia, Indiana Review, Barrow Street*, and others. She was Halls Poetry Fellow at the Wisconsin Institute for Creative Writing in 2005-2006. She is the recipient of a Hopwood Award from the University of Michigan, a James Wright Poetry Award from *Mid-American Review*, and a 2010 grant from the NH State Council on the Arts.